First World War
and Army of Occupation
War Diary
France, Belgium and Germany

15 DIVISION
Divisional Troops
B Squadron 1/1 Westmorland and Cumberland Yeomanry
19 June 1915 - 27 April 1917

WO95/1923/1

The Naval & Military Press Ltd
www.nmarchive.com
Published in association with The National Archives

Published by

The Naval & Military Press Ltd

Unit 10 Ridgewood Industrial Park,

Uckfield, East Sussex,

TN22 5QE England

Tel: +44 (0) 1825 749494

www.naval-military-press.com

www.nmarchive.com

This diary has been reprinted in facsimile from the original. Any imperfections are inevitably reproduced and the quality may fall short of modern type and cartographic standards.

© Crown Copyright
Images reproduced by permission of The National Archives, London, England, 2015.

Contents

Document type	Place/Title	Date From	Date To
Heading	WO95/1923/1		
Heading	15th Division. "B" Squadron Westmoreland & Cumberland Yeomanry Jun 1915-Apl 1916 To II Corps		
Heading	B Sq. West & Cumberl Yeo Vol: 4		
Heading	15th Division. "B" Squadron 1/1 West Cumb: Yeo Vol I June to Oct 15		
War Diary		19/06/1915	01/08/1915
War Diary		28/07/1915	27/09/1915
War Diary	Mazingarbe-Drouvin	28/09/1915	29/09/1915
War Diary	Labuissiere	30/09/1915	02/10/1915
War Diary	Lapugnoy	03/10/1915	09/10/1915
War Diary	Lapugnoy	10/10/1915	14/10/1915
War Diary	To Houchin	15/10/1915	21/10/1915
War Diary	Drouvin	22/10/1915	30/10/1915
Heading	15th Division "B" Sq. West. Cumber: Yeo: Vol 2 Nov 15		
Miscellaneous	To. A.G. Office at Base.	03/12/1915	03/12/1915
War Diary	Drouvin	01/11/1915	30/11/1915
Heading	15th Div. "B" Sq. West Cumberland Yeo. Vol 3 December 1915		
War Diary	Sheet 1	01/12/1915	19/12/1915
War Diary	Sheet 2	20/10/1915	31/10/1915
War Diary	Hurionville	01/01/1916	05/01/1916
War Diary	Beaumetz Les Aire	06/01/1916	06/01/1916
War Diary	Hurionville	07/01/1916	15/01/1916
War Diary	Vaudricourt	15/01/1916	31/01/1916
Heading	B Squadron No. of Yeo.15 Vol. V		
War Diary	Vaudricourt	01/02/1916	25/02/1916
Heading	B Squad West & Cumb Vol 6 15 Dec		
War Diary	Vaudricourt	01/03/1917	26/03/1917
War Diary	Hurionville	27/03/1917	29/03/1917
War Diary		12/03/1917	12/03/1917
War Diary	Therouanne	01/04/1916	01/04/1916
War Diary	Hesdignul Near Samer	02/04/1917	15/04/1917
War Diary	Coyecques	17/04/1917	17/04/1917
War Diary	Hurionville	18/04/1917	23/04/1917
War Diary	Fouquereuil	26/04/1917	27/04/1917
Miscellaneous	O.C. 11th Entrenching Battalion. Gordon Highlanders. Appendix. I	23/06/1916	23/06/1916
Miscellaneous	Headquarters Heavy Artillery 4th Corps.	25/06/1916	25/06/1916
Miscellaneous	To. C.R.E. 2nd Division.	23/06/1916	23/06/1916

145/(3230)

109/1923

15TH DIVISION

'B' SQUADRON WESTMORELAND
& CUMBERLAND YEOMANRY

JUN 1915-APL 1916

To 11 CORPS

"15" Ap: Werk: Hundel, Geo.
Vol: 4

15.

121/7592

15th Division

"B" Squadron 1st West: Kumb: Yeos
Vol I
June to Oct 15
Opn '16

B. Squadron   1/1 West Cumbd Yeomanry
WAR DIARY. June 19 - Oct 31st.   XV Divl Cavalry.

1915 June	
19.	Squadron left the Regiment at Bedford and joined the XV Division at MARLBOROUGH as Divisional Cavalry. Went under canvas ½ mile SW of MARLBOROUGH.
20-23	Squadron training continued.
23.	Marched to WILCOT and bivouaced there with 44th Infy Bde.
24.	Inspected by H.M. King George V near SIDBURY HILL with XV Division, returning to camp at MARLBORO' after inspection.
26.	Inspected by G.O.C. XV Division
27?	Tactical Scheme with Cyclist Co.
July 29-1	Squadron training.
2	Divisional Operations near SWINDON.
4.	Orders for embarkation received. 2 a.m.
5-9.	Fitting out Squadron for service abroad. New saddlery, swords, rifle buckets, transport carts etc drawn & issued. Rifles exchanged.
10	Squadron left MARLBOROUGH & entrained for SOUTHAMPTON arriving there midday. Two trains used. Embarked on SS African Prince & left at 5 p.m.

July 11.	Landed at HAVRE at 9 a.m. Spent the day helping Ammunition column to disembark. Very slow work owing to slow running cranes. Moved to Rest Camp at 4.30.
July 12.	Entrained at 5 pm & moved off at 9 pm All night on train. Horses quiet after first hour. No casualties.
13.	Arrived ST OMER 4 p.m. Detrained & marched to SERQUES. New transport on pavé roads very troublesome.
14	At SERQUES.
15.	Left SERQUES at 6 a.m. & marched to RENESCURE. arriving midday. Men bathed.
16.	Left RENESCURE at 6.15 a m & marched to ECQUEDECQUES. arriving 12.30. In front of division & trotted a good deal. All went well on a long march.
17.	Left ECQUEDECQUES at 9 a m & marched to MARLES LES MINES. Billeted there in barns round the church. Horses in field by river. Good water for men & horses.

MMG Battery had some troubles on march but generally caught up. They came by road from HAVRE & were two days late owing to break downs.

July 18 – 24	At MARLES-LES-MINES. Working at Sword exercise & new rifle buckets. With help of 2 NCO from Northumberland Hussars lent us as instructors. MMG Battery ran a course of MG instruction for Cyclist Coy.
Jul 24.	Took over control post at MARLES from King Edwards Horse. 47th Div Cavalry. 1 officer 15 men.
July 25th Aug 1.	Work for Squadron as before. With Dummy thrusting & jumping added.
Jul 28	2 Lt Burns Lindow & 3 men of Squadron 3 Cyclist Co detached to form Divisional Observation Party. Went away for instruction in duties from 47th Division.
Aug 1st	~~Moved~~ Took over 6 road control Posts round VAUDRICOURT & NOEUX LES MINES from 47th Division. Cyclist Co supply 8 posts beyond NOEUX.
Aug 2.	Moved to VAUDRICOURT at 7 pm, arriving at 9.30 pm. Squadron in two orchards. Men bivouaced. Move carried out in the dark very successfully. MMG Battery moved to VAUDRICOURT Cyclist Co to DROUVIN. 15th Division relieving 47th Div. Relief completed Aug 4th.

4

Aug 2-8. At VAUDRICOURT. Very little water. Best watering at
coal mine near BRUAY, 3 miles away.
  Daily routine, water & exercise in mornings -
    Sword exercise afternoon.
  Road control posts changed every Saturday.
  MMG Battery improving their field & working at
    musketry.
  Cyclist Co supplying fatigues for the Division.

Aug 9-15 At VAUDRICOURT.
  Daily routine. Water & exercise horses in morning.
    4 patrols of four men each sent out every day
    to learn country & roads between our lines &
    trenches. Northumberland Hussar
    NCO's returned.
  MMG Battery manning keep behind front trenches
  Squadron & cyclist improving lines & bivouacs.
  Green food for horses bought from farmers standing
    & parties sent grass cutting daily.
  Horse No 123 of No 3 Troop died of colic on 10th.
  1 Cpl MMG Battery accidentally killed by
    revolver on 7th Aug.

  Capt Lacy (late of B Squadron) attached R E
    killed at CAMBRIN in a mine on Aug 14.
  5 officers & 10 NCO's & men attended his funeral.

16-22
Aug 18-25

At VAUDRICOURT.

Daily routine. Morning water & exercise horses
Afternoon. Work in village clearing roads
    clearing drains & culverts, repairing footpaths
    etc.
Patrols sent out 9-12 pm in evenings to get
    to know roads at night. 16 men each night.
Aug 21. Route march to MARLES les MINES to
    get washed at a mine there.
    Farmers helped to lead corn
A further road control post taken over on this
day. & called No 4A to stop traffic from
VAUDRICOURT - VERQUIN
Horses inspected by Col Hall Walker &
Col Bates D.A.D.R. on Aug 18 & considered in
good condition. They are getting green food
most days & 10 lbs hay. Much troubled with
kicks & consider it bad policy not to issue more
heel shackles. Three cases of ringworm all
arising from service set of saddlery.

MMG Battery manning keep. Started school of
    instruction for M.G. Major Hall appointed Div
    M.G. Officer

Cyclists supplying 8 road control posts, HQ
    guard, & sundry divisional fatigues

Aug 22/29.

At VAUDRICOURT

Daily Routine. Drill 9.15 - 10
 Watch Exercise 10 - 12.
 Cleaning Streets. 2.30-4.30
Grass cutting daily.
A great heap of manure removed from near No 2/4 lines by continual fatigue parties throughout the week.
A great work started on main drain of village with help from Local Road authorities.

Aug 26 Route march to River near MARLES for washing.
New control post at K.4 central started

Aug 27. Posts at NOEUX LES MINES & DROUVIN relieved by 47th Division, which takes over subsection W of trenches & country behind it from Aug 29.

Aug 29. Division takes over mb Section Y.1. Boundaries of area altered but no change of camp for squadron

Strength as at Aug 22.
Pte Lund returned from hospital
Pte Vickers gone to "
Horses well, no fresh ring worms & fewer kicks

Aug 30. – Sep 4.	At Vaudricourt Daily Routine as before. A week of movement for others. Stationary & dull for Squadron.
Sep 1.2	Inspection in full marching order by troops. No 3 easily best. No serious faults or shortages. Transport very bad. Pack saddles in a very disgraceful condition.
Sep 3.	HQS of Division moved from ~~VAUD~~ DROUVIN to VAUDRICOURT. Cyclists to move ditto 47th Division now on our right with 1st Div artillery. 9th Div on our left.

Sep 4	To Bath House at NŒUX LES MINES. Operation order No 7 issued relating to Infantry movements only.
	
	Strength. 2 less than Aug 22.
	    2 Lyraddlers attached to 45th Infy Bde.
	    Heywood to APM as interpreter
	    Lt Bowman & Hutchinson ~~to~~ from Observation duty
	    Weir to " "
	
	No fresh cases to hospital

7

At VAUDRICOURT.

Sep 5 – 11
Daily Routine as before.
Preparation for operations continued but often postponed.

Sep 5
Experimental run of waggons from VERQUIN – FOSSE 7 guided by Div Mtd Troops. Quite successful though over zealous guides interfered with other traffic. Left camp 5.30 & returned 11.30 p.m.

Capt Look of cyclists detached at Bde Major 44th Infy Bde. Richards in command.

Sep 6
7 Nothing of interest
8 Emergency control post called out Sep 8. Turned out
9 in ½ hour but not really wanted.

Sep 10
Made plan of proposed position for Div Cavalry.
Subsequently altered to position for MMG & Cyclists.

Sep 11
Reconnoitred position at NŒUX.
Men wanted at NŒUX.
2 new posts established at VERQUIN & NŒUX.

Cyclists working at bomb school – MMG & Cyclists preparing dug outs. Squadron took on HQ Guard every other day & HQ fatigue daily. (1 NCO & few men)

5 cases Scabies. 5 Diarrhœa.   2 new Ringworm

Sep. 12-18.   AT VAUDRICOURT.

Mon: Routine work. Crossing the country with Squadron
Tues   in extended line of Troop columns.
        Bayonet Exercise etc.

Wed.   With Major Campbell North? Hussars to MAROC.
        owing to idea that we may be grouped together.

Thurs.   Ditto N. VERMELLES.

Frid.y   "   with Major Lockett 11th Hsrs to VERMELLES

Sat   "   "   "   to MAROC.
 18
        Very little with Squadron.
        Guide posts put out to guide convoys. which
        were ~~mens~~ conducted duly to destination.
        32 men from No 2 & 4 Troops did the work
        Left camp 5.30 & returned 12.30. Fine night

        Lydrich & MMG Battery digging themselves
        in at X roads N. of Sandchiry Farm.

        Pte Vickers returned from hospital. 4 men
        absent now & Robson in England.
        Horses well. I never my own on 18th.

        Operation orders No 9.10.11 with reference to great
            attack of 25 issued.

Sep 19-24.	At VAUDRICOURT.
Sep 19.	Continue to escort waggons from VERQUIN to Fosse 7. St Lindon + Div Observers returned to duty.
Sep 21.	First day of bombardment. Troop inspection. Much better turn out than on previous occasions. All control posts relieved.
22.	Second day of bombardment. Same work as above
23.	Third day of bombardment. Squadron parade, cross country work. Largest turn out for many weeks.
24.	Last day of bombardment. Another good squadron parade.

For part taken in operation see over.

Report on Operations. Sep 24-28.
15th Divl Mounted Troops

Sep 24. 8 p.m. Squadron moved up to NOEUX les MINES & bivouaced there.
3 platoons cyclists & M.M.G. battery to dug outs prepared behind MAZINGARBE. O/C Mtd Troops with them.
Remainder of cyclists under A.P.M.

Sep 25. 10.30 a.m. Orders received for 11th M.M.G. Battery to proceed to QUALITY STREET to report to 44 Infy Bde. They are to be moved forward later to Northern outskirts of LOOS at discretion of G.O.C. 44 Infy Bde with a view to support our attack on Hill 70.

In answer to further enquiries they are instructed to take no cyclists with them & to leave F. Trench mortar battery at MAZINGARBE.

They started off at 11.10. The O/C 11th M.M.G. Battery reports their further progress.

11.45. Orders received for Two platoons of cyclists to get ready & for O/C cyclists to report to Divl H.Q.S.

They started off about midday. O/C Cyclists reports their further progress.

11.50. Orders received for squadron to move up to join me at MAZINGARBE.

They arrived at 1.30 having been much hindered on roads full of cavalry & supporting troops.

Report on Operations Sep 24-28   Sheet 2.
11

12.0 midday. Thousands of cavalry pass between
NOYELLES & MAZINGARBE - Continuous stream for
more than an hour.
  21st Division begins to arrive from NOEUX les
MINES & form up just in L.16 b & L 16 c
just behind our position. & halt there.

  Squadron complete & one platoon of cyclists stand by
12 midnight for orders for remainder of day.   (LOOS
  Trench mortar was ordered to report to 46 Inf Bde

Sep 26. 11.30 a.m. Remaining platoon of cyclists sent for to
                assist battle police.

  12 midday. One troop of cavalry ordered to report to
              APM for escort & road control work. Despatched
              No 1 Troop at 12.15. They remained out till
              6 pm Sept 27th.

  4 pm. Orders received that remainder of squadron
        is to go out & work under 44th Inf Bde dismounted.
        Rode up to Fosse 7 & sent back horses from
        there. Report to 44th Inf Bde in QUALITY STREET
        at 5.15 pm. with 57 men.

  6.15 pm. Carry entrenching tools to O/C 7th
           Camerons & 10th Gordons. Take up 100 picks &
           100 shovels in two journeys to original German
           trenches at on LENS road.

Report on Operation Sept 24-28.   sheet 3
                                    12

8 pm. Carry rations to Bde Bde Headquarters
       and send party with rations to 10th Gordons
       in old German trenches near LENS road.

10 pm. Unload a lorry of smoke helmets at
        RE Stores, Quality Street.

Midnight. CRE asks for 20 men to assist in
           repairing LENS road send troop up under
           2.Lt Burns Lindow.

Sep 29. 2.30 a.m. Orders received at Bde HQS that the
         Division is to come out to billets in MAZINGARBE.
         Marched back to dugouts at L 17.c. arriving
         there at 4 a.m.

9. a.m. Find MMG battery has returned during
         our absence.
         O/C Cyclist Co with two platoons returns
         during the morning.

6 pm. No Troop return from APM. also
       platoon of cyclists.

10 pm. Sent for to Divl HQS. & receive orders to be
        ready to move at 1 hours notice with all
        available Mounted Troops. Order cancelled
Sep 28. at 9.30 a.m Sep 29. & Mtd Troops ordered
        to march to billets at DROUVIN.

Report on Operation Sep 26-28   Sheet 13

Sep 27. 12.30 a.m. Ordered to send out two officers patrols to find position of captured German field guns in LOOS.

2nd Lts Robinson & Burns Lindow went out but found themselves in the middle of the Guards Division who were advancing towards LOOS & were unable to make progress before dark. They returned not having discovered the guns, having been held up by the heavy bombardment directed against the Guards Division till the light gave out.

They were instructed to be ready to start again at dawn but the orders were subsequently cancelled.

Sep 28 – Oct 2   14

Sep 28. MAZINGARBE – DROUVIN. Left MAZINGARBE at 12.15
         and arrived in DROUVIN at 2.30. Men
         billeted in barns.

Sep 29. A day of contradictory orders. Ordered first to move
         from DROUVIN. Then to stay there. Then
         finally had to clear out to make room for infantry
         going up to front.
         Left DROUVIN in pouring rain at 5 pm &
         marched to LABUISSIERE. arriving 6.30 pm &
         getting into billets about 8.30.

Sep 30. At LABUISSIERE. Moved horses from a muddy
         ploughed field into grass. Wet day.

Oct. 1. Gen Sir H Rawlinson GOC 4th Corps addressed
         45th Brigade & Mtd Troops at LABUISSIERE.
         & complimented them on operation of
         Sept 25/6/7.
         Squadron watered at HALLENCOURT mine &
         had a good trot round.

Oct 2.   Maj Gen McCracken addressed Mtd Troops in
         LABUISSIERE.
         Major Cropper sick. Maj Hall in command.

Oct 3 - 9.

~~At Labuissiere~~
~~Oct 2nd~~ ~~My Gen McCracken addressed Mtd~~

Oct 3. Received orders to move to LAPUGNOY, & to be clear of billets in LABUISSIERE by 1 pm.
Many troops on the move & progress very slow arrived LAPUGNOY at 4 pm.

Oct 4. LAPUGNOY
Settling into new billets. Men in one large barn. Horses by river. good water. & handy. Artillery all round us.

Oct 5. Route march to BURBURE. & back by BETHUNE road & ALLOUAGNE. 2 Troops doing protection on flanks. 1st line Transport did better than usual but only carried half loads. Heavy Rain at times.
3 Remounts drawn.

Oct 6. Troop parades.
MMG Battery started a school of instruction.
Cyclists company wanted for a few days but had to supply a post at MARLES.
Leave granted, 3 per day for Mtd Troops
Major Cropper Capt Locke & Lieut Anderson went 1st day.

Oct 7/8 Lt Hunter & de Romignol joined MMG Battery
9 Leave stopped. 7 Lt Robinson SSM Gundall got away before stoppage.

Oct 10 - 16.

LAPUGNOY.

Oct 10. Op Orders No 12. rec'd. Div'n to move. Mtd Troops on one hour's notice after Oct 11. Subsequently altered to Oct 12.

Oct 11. Corps orders received to mend roads, work apportioned between units & done.

Oct 12 Op Orders No 13 received. Div'n moving. Mtd Troops remain at LAPUGNOY on 1 hour's notice. No special work possible under these circumstances.

Oct 14. Major Cropper returned from leave.
Op Orders No 14 received. Mtd Troops to move to HOUCHIN. Move to be completed by noon.

Oct 15 To <u>HOUCHIN</u>. Very crowded there, but got men into barns. Water difficult but some a mile away. Only very deep wells & slow work. Lt Robinson from leave.
Cavalry took over 2 control posts. Cyclists 3.

Oct 16 MMG Battery to HALLICOURT.
Leave granted again but only 1 per day to Mtd Troops. Maj Hall MMG went 17:00.
SSM Grindal from leave.
Cavalry took over another control post.

Oct 17 - 23.
HOUCHIN

Oct 17. Church parade Drouvin Chateau.
Major Cropper + Lt Lindow visited LOOS & found bombarded trenches impossible for horses.

Oct 18 Cyclist sent a control post to MAZINGARBE.
Jumping practice in morning.
Sergt Noble started Leave.

Oct 19. All control posts round NOEUX relieved by infantry. Cavalry left with one post.

Oct 20. 2Lt Burns Lindow went on leave. Leave reduced to 1 every 3rd day for M.M Troops.

21 ~~Troops to~~ Dismounted attack in afternoon
Troop parades changing from Yeomanry to Cavalry drill.
Night operation 5.30 - 7.30.

DROUVIN

22 Squadron moved to DROUVIN Billeted in old chateau there.

23 Arranging lines and settling into new billets
Squadron went to baths at BRUAY.
Sent a fatigue party to A.S.C. to load coal.
Cyclists working for R.E. in trenches west of week. M.M.G. battery running MG school at HAILLICOURT.

DROUVIN.
Oct 24 – 30.

Oct 24. Church Parade at Chateau.

25. Wet day. Exercise horses morning. Clean up horses in afternoon.
Cyclists to trenches.

26. Squadron parade doing Cavalry method of increasing & diminishing front.

27. One troop No 3 go to trenches to collect telephone wire for Signal Co.
4th control post put onto cavalry. 28 dismounted men out.
20 men forming party to clear roads for H.M. the King who came to inspect IV & XI Corp.

28. No 3 Troop Wire clearing.
No 4 Troop to cut up wood for charcoal burning near LAPUGNOY.
No 1 & 2 very short of men, exercise horse.

29. No 3 Troop wire clearing
30. No 4 Wood cutting.

30. 5 control posts cleared 2 taken over by M.M.G. battery No 3 & No 4 troop resting.

15th Division

"B" dep: rest: number, &c:
vol: 2

121/7694

Nov 15

To A.G's Office at Base.

Herewith War Diary for November
for 15th Divisional Cavalry.

3/12/15.

W Cropper Major

Army Form C. 2118.

WAR DIARY
or
INTELLIGENCE SUMMARY.
(Erase heading not required.)

Instructions regarding War Diaries and Intelligence Summaries are contained in F. S. Regs., Part II. and the Staff Manual respectively. Title pages will be prepared in manuscript.

Place	Date	Hour	Summary of Events and Information	Remarks and references to Appendices
DROUVIN	1/11/15		2 Troops working with 46th Bde Signals clearing disused Telephone from trenches. 1 Troop cutting wood for charcoal. 2 Patrol control Posts supplied by squadron. 6 men attached Signal Co as despatch riders.	
"	2/11/15		Ordered to find patrols to watch reserve line of Trenches. Party of N.C.O.s taken round French reserve line. 1 Troop clearing mine. 1 Troop cutting.	
"	3/11/15		Trench patrols started work. Ordered to have two orderlies standing by daily to General Staff when visiting trenches.	
"	4/5/6 & 7/11/15.		Work as above. Mine clearing. Woodcutting & Trench Patrols. 2 Control Posts relieved by bicyclists on 5th.	
"	Nov 7/8		Same work as previous week.	
	/9		Woodcutting fatigue finished its work.	
	/11		1 Control Post near DROUVIN taken over from cyclists. Hd Divisional Headquarters moved to VAUDRICOURT Nov 10	
	/12		Ordered to supply a Guard for Divisional Headquarters Daily.	
	Nov 14/20.		Work throughout week. 8 men with Brigade Signals Co working on buried Telephone line in Trenches. 6 as despatch riders with HQS Signal Co. 4 men as Control Post. 1 Officer + 1 man Observation duty. 4 men Headquarters Guard. 2 men Two Orderlies for Staff Officer. 16 men daily on Trench Patrols.	

T2134. Wt. W708—776. 500000. 4/15. Sir J. C. & S.

WAR DIARY
or
INTELLIGENCE SUMMARY.

Army Form C. 2118.

Place	Date	Hour	Summary of Events and Information	Remarks and references to Appendices
DROUVIN	Nov 21-27		Work as previous week.	
	Nov 25		Divisional area changed, ours extends to North taken in. One control post relieved + two more taken on.	
	Nov 28-30		Observation Party increased to 4 men, 1 officer; men billeted at NOYELLES.	
			Work. 8 men with Signal boys clearing telephone line.	
			6 men with HQ Signal Co.	
			1 officer + 6 men Observation Party.	
			8 men on Control Posts.	
			4 men HQ Guard.	
			12 men daily, Trench Patrol.	

Wilespie Major
MAJOR, O.C.
15TH DIVISIONAL CAVALRY

"B" Sq: West: Cumberland: Yeo:

Vol. 3

121/7868

December 1915.

WAR DIARY or INTELLIGENCE SUMMARY

Army Form C. 2118.

Place	Date	Hour	Summary of Events and Information	Remarks and references to Appendices
West	December 1915		B Squadron 1/1 Westmoreland & Cumberland Yeomanry. 1st Divisional Cavalry.	
	Dec. 1. 1915		Squadron stationed at Chateau DROUVIN. Men following detachment.	
			8 men working on telephone wire for Brigade Signal Co. in communication trenches. Stationed at NOYELLES.	
			6 men working for HQ Signal Co. as despatch riders. Stationed at VAUDRICOURT.	
			1 officer + 6 men acting as orderlies. Stationed at SAILLY LA BOURSE & NOYELLES.	
			8 men as examining control posts at VERQUIN & VERQUIGNEUL.	
			Daily duties. Lines to Vaudricourt Chateau for Divisional Headquarters Guard.	
			12 men as patrols to watch reserve line of trenches.	
	Dec 2.		1 officer + 12 men to trenches to make shelters for observing party.	
	" 7.		12 men ordered by HQS for a fatigue to load coal.	
	"13/14		14 men + 1 officer each day to patrol roads for 47th Division moving in from Corps Reserve.	
	13.		8 men from Brigade Signal Co. returned to duty.	
	14.		14 men to control posts at MARLES les MINES & LOZINGHEM. Posts at VERQUIN & VERQUIGNEUL relieved by 47th Div.	
	15.		Squadron moved to HURIONVILLE. 2nd in 'Seq' LILLERS. Division into Corps Reserve. Divisional HQS to Chateau PHILOMEL. LILLERS. Observation party rejoined Squadron.	
	19.		Patrolled roads for passage of Sir John French.	

Army Form C. 2118.

WAR DIARY
or
INTELLIGENCE SUMMARY.
(Erase heading not required.)

Place	Date	Hour	Summary of Events and Information	Remarks and references to Appendices
Sheet 2.	December 1915.		B.Squadron "I" Westmorland & Cumberland Yeomanry. 15th Divisional Cavalry.	
	Dec 20.		Tactical Exercise for Divisional Mounted Troops.	
	25.		Eastern Posts at MARLES-LOZINGHEM relieved by Cyclist Co.	
	26.		Half Squadron shoot musketry course at BURBURE.	
	22.		Four men from H.Q. Signal Co returned to duty.	
	31.		Eastern Posts at MARLES & LOZINGHEM taken over by Squadron.	

W.Cooper Major
15TH DIVISIONAL CAVALRY

Sheet. 1.

Army Form C. 2118.

B. Sqn: 1/1 Westmoreland & Cumberland Yeo: 15th Divisional Cavalry.

WAR DIARY
or
INTELLIGENCE SUMMARY.

for January 1916.

(Erase heading not required.)

Instructions regarding War Diaries and Intelligence Summaries are contained in F. S. Regs., Part II. and the Staff Manual respectively. Title pages will be prepared in manuscript.

Place	Date	Hour	Summary of Events and Information	Remarks and references to Appendices
HURIONVILLE.	Jan 1.		Troop Training.	
	" 2.		No 1 & 2 Troop fired Musketry Course.	
	" 3/4		Troop Training.	
	" 5		Divisional Exercise. Division marched East from LILLERS by LIETTRES, AUCHY au BOIS, CUHEM, BOMY. Mtd Troop formed vanguard to Advanced Guard. On arrival at BOMY ordered to hold outpost line West of PETIGNY till 3:30 when relieved by infantry & went to billets at BEAUMETZ lès AIRE.	
BEAUMETZ lès AIRE.	6.		Division ordered to move in 3 columns & take up defensive position on high ground between LYS & AA Rivers. Mtd Troop to cover their advance to position. Position abandoned at 2 p.m. Mtd Troop to cover retirement & posting of outpost line West of PETIGNY. Returned to billets at BEAUMETZ at 4 p.m.	
"	"			
HURIONVILLE.	7.		Division ordered to march West. Mounted Troop to form vanguard & support to Advance Guard. 10 mile march to starting point at 8:30. Returned to billets at HURIONVILLE.	
	8.		Cleaning up & resting after Divisional Exercise.	
	9/10/11.		Training in conjunction with Cyclist Company.	
	12		Equipment lorries, 1 Gunner, 1 signalman, 1 officer, 16 men to take over divisional park from 1st Division.	
	13/14/15.		Road control for troops of 1st & 15th Division during relief.	

Sheet 2

B Squadron 1/1 Westmorland & Cumberland Yeomanry.

WAR DIARY or **INTELLIGENCE SUMMARY**

Army Form C. 2118.

m Jan. 1916.

(Erase heading not required.)

Place	Date	Hour	Summary of Events and Information	Remarks and references to Appendices
	January			
VAUDRICOURT.	15.		Squadron moved from HURIONVILLE to VAUDRICOURT.	
	16.		6 men to HQS Signal Co to work on despatch riders.	
	–		3 men added to Stevenson party to work on Telephones.	
	17/18/19.		Troop drill at VERQUIN.	
	20.		1 Officer & 30 men ordered to go daily to NOEUX les MINES to work on huts/tents under R.E.	
	23.		Inspection & competition. No fatigue found.	
	24/31.		Fatigue party daily to NOEUX les MINES. Remainder of Squadron exercising horses.	

JWCropper
MAJOR, O.C.
16TH DIVISIONAL CAVALRY

B Squadron
W. of. Yeo. 15
Vol V

H. G. James

1. Bt. Tryardun, 1/1 Westmorland & Cumberland Yeomanry. 1st Divisional Cavalry.

WAR DIARY for month of February.

or

INTELLIGENCE SUMMARY.

(Erase heading not required.)

Army Form C. 2118.

Place	Date	Hour	Summary of Events and Information	Remarks and references to Appendices
VAUDRICOURT	Feb 1.		12 men attached to Divisional dispatch to lay a cable from MAZINGARBE - LOOS. Billeted at PHILOSOPHE.	
	8.		20 men & 1 officer daily to huts at NOEUX LES MINES.	
	12.		Cable laying party returned. Party to hutment at NOEUX increased to 30 men.	
			Special instructions received as to procedure on signal GAS ALERT being received from D.H.Q.	
	18		2nd Lt Robinson attached to 112 M.M.G. Battery to take charge of section in front line trenches.	
	21.		2nd Lt M.Burns Lindow returned from A.D.C. to G.O.C. 15th Divn by Capt G Carleton Cowper.	
	24		2nd Lt Raymond on leave to England. 2nd Lt M.Burns-Lindow to observation party.	
	25		2nd Lt Robinson to England to report to O/C M.G. Training Centre, GRANTHAM.	
			"Daily Morgan transport the work has been 30 men to hutments at NOEUX-LES-MINES. 10 men & 1 officer on renovation duty. 6 men attached signal to an despatch riders. Remainder at work with horses at VAUDRICOURT, &c. position employ —	

Wolcough.
MAJOR, O.C.
1/1TH WESTMORLAND CUMBERLAND

B Seward
Westcomb
Vol 6 / 3
1st D

B Squadron 1/1 West Kent Yeomanry, 1st Div Cavalry.

WAR DIARY or INTELLIGENCE SUMMARY.

Army Form C. 2118.

for March 1916.

(Erase heading not required.)

Place	Date	Hour	Summary of Events and Information	Remarks and references to Appendices
VAUDRICOURT	Mar 1–16		2 officers + 12 men on observation duty for Division	
			6 men attached to ? put to an despatch riders	
			6 others on Divisional Employment.	
			Fatigue party of 30 men daily to build huts at NOEUX-LES-MINES.	
			Remainder of squadron exercising horses + map reading classes.	
	Mar 6		4 men to be kept ready to act as guides for reinforcements to front line	
	Mar 16/17		Fatigue party finished. Squadron drill for first time since October. Musketry on range in afternoon. 89 men fired a short course.	
	18		Tactical Exercise with MMG Battery	
	19		2nd Lt JENKINS joined Squadron from D Squadron (20th Dn Cavalry)	
	21		Lt BURNS-LINDOW left Squadron to be adjt to 20th Div Mtd Troops.	
			Tactical Exercise for Cavalry in BOIS DES DAMES.	
	23		Tactical Exercise with Cyclists + MMG Battery under supervision of Divisional + Corps Staff.	
	25/26/27		Traffic control for Division moving into Reserve area	
	26		Observation Party returned to Squadron	

B Squadron "West Yeomanry 1st Div'l Cavalry."

WAR DIARY
or
INTELLIGENCE SUMMARY.

Army Form C. 2118.

(Erase heading not required.)

Instructions regarding War Diaries and Intelligence Summaries are contained in F. S. Regs., Part II. and the Staff Manual respectively. Title pages will be prepared in manuscript.

Place	Date	Hour	Summary of Events and Information	Remarks and references to Appendices
HURIONVILLE	Mar 27		Squadron moved to HURIONVILLE.	
	28		Orders received that Squadron & Cyclists are to be attached to 1st Cavalry Division for training from April 1–17.	
	29		Squadron & Cyclists inspected by G.O.C. 1st Division. Signal despatch riders returned to Squadron.	
	Mar 12		During month 3 men have left Twin Expired. known to England on result of an injury Lt. F.C. PARKER attached to England to report to Secretary War Office.	

J. Whippe
Major

B West & Cum

Army Form C. 2118.
V017

B Squadron 1/1 West & Lmtd Yeomanry – 1st Divisional Cavalry –
WAR DIARY
or
1st April 1916
INTELLIGENCE SUMMARY.
(Erase heading not required.)

XV
XII

Place	Date	Hour	Summary of Events and Information	Remarks and references to Appendices
THEROUANNE.	April 1st		Marched to THEROUANNE from LILLERS on way to join 1st Cavalry Division. Cyclist Company with us.	
HESDIGNEUL near SAMER.	2.		Marched to SAMER reported to 1st Cavalry Division - sent on to billets at HESDIGNEUL. Reported to the Mounted Troops School of Instruction	
	3 to 15.		Work under Capt Nicholson 13th Hussars at School of Instruction. On April 5th 2Lt H.M. GIBSON + 2nd Lt A.R.J. OYSTER joined Squadron from No 5 far Base Depot. On April 8th Capt Bowman T. went to course of instruction on Hotchkiss Gun.	
COYECQUES.	17.		Return march from 1st Cav: Div: HESDIGNEUL – COYECQUES. 30 miles.	
HURIONVILLE.	18.		March continued to HURIONVILLE. Reported to XV Division. Division attemperat on GHQ Reserve	
	23.		2 Lt Raymond + 10 men left to take over Observation duty from 12th Division	
FOUQUEREUIL	26.		Squadron marched to FOUQUEREUIL. 15th Division relieving 12th Division in HOHENZOLLERN sector.	
	27.		Gas attack on front near HULLUCH. Gas guide attem at FOUQUEREUIL but helmet not necessary. Squadron asked to stand to but no developments. Attack dealt with by 16th Division on our right.	
			During the month 3 men left the Squadron, Discharged on Time Expiring. 3 men were evacuated Draft of 4 men received. + 2 officers. Strength on April 30. 6 officers. 125 other ranks	

N.C. Copper
Major. O.I.C.
1/1st DIVISIONAL CAVALRY

T2134. Wt. W708—776. 500000. 4/15. Sir J.C. & S.

APPENDIX I

O.C.
    11th Entrenching Battalion.
    Gordon Highlanders.

IVth Corps No.24616(G)
Gen Staff.

    I forward attached copy of letter received from the G.O.C.R.A.IV Corps with regard to the good work done by your Battalion.

    The Chief Engineer IV Corps also reports that your Battalion has done very good work all through.

    The Corps Commander wishes me to bring this to your notice and to express his gratification at the reports received.

(signed) H.de Pree
Brigadier General
General Staff IVth Corps.

H.Q.
24th June 1916.

Headquarters,
    IVth Corps.

1.   I desire to place on record the good work done by the company of "11th Provisional Battalion of the Gordon Highlanders" which has been attached to IV Corps Heavy Artillery for entrenching purposes.

2.   On the augmentation of the Corps Heavy Artillery between 23rd May and 1st June this Company prepared positions in the neighbourhood of BULLY GRENAY with great skill and industry. Without their assistance we should have had great difficulty in getting the guns into action in time to take part in the bombardment of the 1st June.

3.   They also rapidly repaired gun positions which had been heavily shelled by the enemy.

    Their good work has, without doubt, saved many casualties to the Heavy Artillery and their guns.

(signed) J.G.Geddes.
Brigadier General
Commanding R.A. IV Corps.

23rd June 1916.

Headquarters
Heavy Artillery 4th Corps.   4th Army Corps H.A.
                                        No 641.
                                   4th Corps   No.9343.A.

O.C."D"Company 11th Entrenching Battalion has reported to me this morning that his men have been ordered as a draft to some unit. This Company has been attached to 15th Group H.A. for the past few weeks for the purpose of building Battery positions.

I wish to express my great appreciation for the excellent work carried out by the men and for the very ready co-operation of the Officers.

On several occasions when we called on parties of this Company to work by day and by night our orders were carried out with the greatest goodwill.

In conclusion I wish to specially mention the ready co-operation that has been shown by Major A.V.Angus and Captain R.G.Longman.

    (signed) R.H.McCulloch. Lieut Col. R.G.A.
   Commanding 15th Heavy Artillery Group.

15th
H.A.Group.
No.A/177.
23/6/16.

2.

4th Corps.

  Forwarded. I fully concur with Col McCulloch's remarks.

      signed. Brig.Gen.
   Commanding 4th Corps. H.A.
24/6/16.

O.C.11th Entrenching Battalion.

  The Corps Commandant has much satisfaction in forwarding the above letter to you to see.

    (signed) A.C.Jeffcoat Major
    D.A.A.& Q.M.G. 4th Corps.
25/6/16.

To. C.R.E.
    2nd Division.
E.A.546.   23/6/16.

Reference the "C" Company 11th Entrenching Battalion. This Company was withdrawn today and their tools are being collected tomorrow.

I should like to draw attention to the good work done by this Company while under my supervision.

The Officers and men were dependable and very satisfactory work was accomplished.

(signed) F. Wilson.
East Anglean R.E.

2nd Div.

For information. Perhaps you might like to pass to the Battalion.

(signed) C.M. Browne.
Bt. Lieut Col.
A/C.R.E. 2nd Div.

24/6/16

11th Entrenching Bn.

Attached is forwarded for your information. Delay in forwarding is regretted.

(signed) J.D. Belgrave   Major
2nd Division.

5/7/16.